Simply Sensational™

Mexican Recipes

GOLDEN WEST ☼ PUBLISHERS

ISBN #1-885590-28-8

Printed in the United States of America

Golden West Publishers, Inc.
4113 N. Longview Ave.
Phoenix, AZ 85014, USA
(602) 265-4392

Table of Contents

Breakfast

Huevos Rancheros con Frijoles Refritos 7

Huevos Revueltos 8

Burritos por Desayuno 9

Green Chile Omelet 10

Green Chile Salsa 11

Red Chile Salsa 11

Appetizers

Mexican Roll-ups 12

Chile Cheese Nachos 13

Poquitos 13

Guacamole Spread 14

Guacamole Dip 15

Mexicali Bean Dip 16

Soups

Sopa de Pollo Verde 17
Albondigas 18
Sopa de Frijoles Negros 19
Posole 20
Pinto Bean Soup 20

Salads

Ensalada de Frijoles 21
Ensalada de Pollo 21
Ensalada Mexicanos 22
Tres Frijoles Ensalada 23
Ensalada de Verduras..24

Breads

Sopaipillas 25
Mexican Spoon Bread 26
Pan de Frijoles 27

Main Dishes

Enchilada Casserole 28
Chile Verde con Carne 29
Chicken Enchiladas 30
Beef Tacos 31
Tamales 32
Salsa Fria and Barbecued Rib Steaks 34
Frijoles de Ranchero 35
Chili Con Carne 36
Chili Beef 37
Chili Beef Tortilla Casserole 37
Mexican Cabbage Rolls 38
Stuffed Bell Peppers 40
Enchiladas Sabrosos 41
Chalupa para Tostadas y Burros 42
Burros de Chile Verde 43
Fajitas de Pollo 44

Side Dishes

Arroz y Frijoles 45
Chiles Rellenos 46
Eggplant de Mexico 48
Fried Eggplant 49
Frijoles Refritos con Queso 49
Calabacitas con Puerco 50
Mexicali Garbanzos 51

Desserts & Beverages

Fruit Empanadas 52
Flan 53
Dulce Mexicano 54
Mexican Wedding
   Cakes 55
Almendrado 56

Capirotada 58
Dulcitas 59
Polvarones de Lemón 60
Horchata de Melón 61
Chocolate de
   Mexico 62

Huevos Rancheros
con Frijoles Refritos

1 cup GREEN CHILE SALSA
4 oz. LONGHORN CHEESE
4 CORN TORTILLAS
4 EGGS
1 can (16 oz.) REFRIED BEANS
OIL and BUTTER

In a skillet, dip tortillas quickly in heated oil and place each on a baking pan to keep warm. In another skillet, fry eggs in butter until whites are set but yolks are still soft. Heat refried beans and layer on the tortillas. Place an egg on top of beans and spoon *Green* or *Red Chile Salsa* over all (see page 11). Sprinkle with cheese and place under broiler until cheese melts.

Huevos Revueltos
(Scrambled Eggs)

1/4 cup diced ONION
1 can (4 oz.) diced GREEN CHILES, drained
6 EGGS
4 slices cooked BACON, crumbled
SALT and PEPPER to taste

In a medium skillet, sauté onion. Add chiles and bacon to onions and heat. Beat eggs and add to skillet mixture. Add salt and pepper. Cook until set. Serve with salsa and warmed flour tortillas!

Variation: Crush tortilla chips and add to egg mixture just before serving.

Burritos por Desayuno

(Breakfast Burritos)

4 (7") FLOUR TORTILLAS
8 EGGS
1 can (4 oz.) diced GREEN CHILES, drained
1 cup chopped TOMATO
1 cup grated MONTEREY JACK CHEESE
SALT and PEPPER

Warm tortillas and set aside. Combine beaten eggs and chiles and scramble. Place mixture on tortillas, add tomatoes; top with cheese; sprinkle with salt and pepper. Roll up each tortilla burrito style and serve with salsa on the side.

Green Chile Omelet

4 EGGS, beaten
4 Tbsp. MILK
1 can (4 oz.) diced GREEN CHILES
1/2 cup CHEDDAR CHEESE

Combine eggs and milk and beat until creamy. Pour into a pre-heated non-stick skillet. When eggs have "set" add chiles and cheese, then fold and cook until done.

Green Chile Salsa

1 can (16 oz.) diced TOMATOES
1 can (4 oz.) diced CHILES
2 ONIONS, diced
2 cloves GARLIC, crushed

1 Tbsp. CHILI POWDER
1/2 tsp. SALT
1 Tbsp. WHITE VINEGAR

Combine ingredients thoroughly, cover and refrigerate for several hours.

Red Chile Salsa

Same as the *Green Chile Salsa* recipe above except: substitute **2 cans (8 oz. ea.) TOMATO SAUCE** for the tomatoes; do not include the green chiles and increase the chili powder to 2 tablespoons.

Mexican Roll-ups

1 pkg. (8 oz.) CREAM CHEESE, softened
1 pt. (16 oz.) SOUR CREAM
1 can (4 oz.) diced GREEN CHILES, drained
1/2 tsp. GARLIC POWDER
1 lb. LONGHORN CHEESE, grated
1 can (4 oz.) BLACK OLIVES, diced
12 (10-12") FLOUR TORTILLAS

Mix all ingredients together and chill. Spread mixture on tortillas. Begin to roll tortilla, starting with edge closest to you. When all tortillas are filled and rolled, cover and chill well before slicing. Serve with picante or taco sauce.

Chile Cheese Nachos

TORTILLA CHIPS
1/2 cup shredded CHEDDAR CHEESE

1/2 cup shredded JACK CHEESE
1 can (4 oz.) diced GREEN CHILES

Cover a large (12") oven-proof platter with tortilla chips. Sprinkle cheese over top and bake in 350° oven until cheese melts. Top with green chiles and serve with salsa.

Poquitos

8 (10") FLOUR TORTILLAS
8 oz. grated LONGHORN CHEESE

1 cup sliced BLACK OLIVES, drained

Place tortilla on cutting surface. Cut a 2-3" circle from tortilla with a cookie cutter. Cover circles with cheese and garnish with black olives. Place on cookie sheet and broil until cheese is melted.

Guacamole Spread

2 AVOCADOS
1 TOMATO, diced
2 Tbsp. finely chopped ONIONS
1 can (4 oz.) diced GREEN CHILE
1 1/2 Tbsp. WINE VINEGAR
SALT and PEPPER to taste

Mash avocados and combine with balance of ingredients. Makes about 2 cups. Serve with crackers or tortilla chips.

Guacamole Dip

1 lg. AVOCADO
1 med. TOMATO, finely chopped
2 Tsp. grated ONION
1 tsp. LEMON JUICE
1/2 tsp. SALT
1/8 tsp. PEPPER
1/8 tsp. GARLIC POWDER
1 cup SOUR CREAM

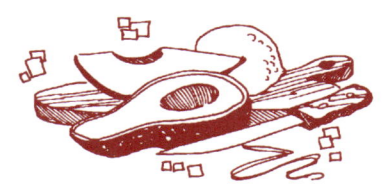

Peel and pit avocado. Mash with a fork. In a bowl, combine all ingredients except sour cream. Stir in sour cream, cover and refrigerate.

Mexicali Bean Dip

2 cans (9 oz. ea.) BEAN DIP
1 cup (8 oz.) SOUR CREAM
1 pkg. (8 oz.) CREAM CHEESE
1 pkg. TACO SEASONING MIX
20 drops TABASCO®
1 cup diced GREEN ONIONS
3 Tbsp. chopped BLACK OLIVES
1/2 cup shredded CHEDDAR CHEESE
TORTILLA CHIPS

In a medium mixing bowl, add all ingredients together with the exception of the cheese and chips. Blend with beater. Pour into ungreased glass baking dish. Sprinkle cheese on top to cover mixture. Bake in 350° oven until hot and cheese is melted. Serve warm with tortilla chips.

Sopa de Pollo Verde

(Chicken Soup with Green Chiles)

1 lb. CHICKEN
4 cups CHICKEN STOCK
4 CELERY STALKS, sliced
1 ONION, sliced
1 Tbsp. FRESH GARLIC, chopped
1 can (4 oz.) diced GREEN CHILES
1 tsp. CUMIN

1/2 tsp. CORIANDER
1/2 tsp. OREGANO
1 cup WATER
2/3 cup CORNSTARCH
SALT and PEPPER, to taste
TORTILLA STRIPS

Remove fat and skin from chicken. Add chicken to chicken stock and boil. Add the next seven ingredients to stock. Cook until chicken and vegetables are done. In a small bowl, combine water and cornstarch and stir until blended. Add cornstarch mixture to soup and stir until it reaches desired consistency. Salt and pepper to taste. Garnish with tortilla strips. Serves 8.

Albondigas
(Meatballs)

Sauce:
- 1 Tbsp. OIL
- 1 ONION, chopped
- 2 cans (8 oz.) TOMATO SAUCE
- 1 cup WATER
- SALT and PEPPER

Sauté onions in hot oil. Add tomato sauce, water, salt and pepper. Cook on very low heat for 15 minutes.

Meat Balls:
- 1 lb. GROUND BEEF
- 1/2 lb. GROUND PORK
- 1 slice BREAD, crumbled
- 3 GREEN ONIONS, chopped
- 1 Tbsp. chopped MINT LEAVES
- 1 EGG

Combine all ingredients. Mix thoroughly and shape into very small balls. Add meatballs to sauce. Cover and cook over medium heat for 40 minutes.

Sopa de Frijoles Negros

(Black Bean Soup)

2 cans (15 oz. ea.) BLACK BEANS, drained
2 cans (14 oz. ea.) CHICKEN STOCK
1/2 cup chopped ONION
1 can (4 oz.) diced GREEN CHILES
1/2 cup DRY SHERRY
SALT and PEPPER, to taste

Combine black beans, chicken stock and onion in saucepan and bring to a boil. Cover and simmer on low heat until onion is tender. Stir in chiles, sherry and salt and pepper and heat for two minutes. Top with a dollop of sour cream.

Posole

1 med. ONION, diced
1 tsp. GARLIC SALT
1 1/2 lbs. ground PORK
3 Tbsp. OIL

1 tsp. ground CUMIN
1 tsp. dried OREGANO
1 can (4 oz.) diced GREEN CHILE
1 can (15 oz.) HOMINY

In a skillet, heat oil and sauté onion, garlic salt, pork and spices. Cook until meat is no longer pink. Add hominy (including juice) and chiles. Cover skillet and simmer for 30 minutes.

Pinto Bean Soup

2 cans (15 oz.) PINTO BEANS
2 cups diced cooked HAM
1 ONION, diced

1 tsp. GARLIC PEPPER
1 cup TOMATO JUICE
4 cups WATER

Combine all ingredients and simmer for 30 minutes.

Ensalada de Frijoles
(Bean Salad)

1 can (15 oz.) BLACK
    BEANS, drained
3 hard boiled EGGS, chopped
1 stalk CELERY, chopped

1/3 cup chopped RED ONION
1/2 cup cubed CHEDDAR
    CHEESE
LETTUCE

Combine all of the ingredients (except lettuce). At serving time, toss with salad dressing of your choice and serve on a bed of lettuce.

Ensalada de Pollo
(Chicken Salad)

1 cup cooked, cubed CHICKEN
1 AVOCADO, cubed
1 med. TOMATO, diced

1 tsp. LEMON JUICE
1 Tbsp. SALSA
LETTUCE

Toss all ingredients together and serve on a bed of lettuce.

Ensalada Mexicanos

(Mexican Salad)

2 lg. GREEN BELL PEPPERS, diced
1 med. ONION, diced
4 med. TOMATOES, diced
1/2 cup CELERY, chopped
4 slices BACON, fried and crumbled
3 hard cooked EGGS, sliced
1/2 tsp. SALT
1 tsp. CHILI POWDER
1/2 cup VINEGAR

Toss together green peppers, onion, tomato, celery, bacon, eggs and salt. Heat chili powder and vinegar to boiling and pour over all. Toss lightly and serve on a bed of lettuce. Serves 6.

Tres Frijoles Ensalada
(Three Bean Salad)

2 cups cooked KIDNEY BEANS
2 cups cooked BLACK BEANS
2 cups cooked GARBANZO BEANS
1 thinly sliced RED ONION
1 stalk CELERY, sliced
1 TOMATO, diced
1 cup THICK & CHUNKY SALSA
shredded LETTUCE

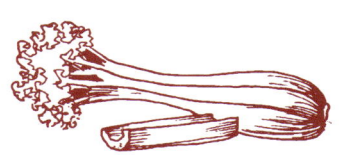

Combine all of the ingredients (except lettuce) in a large bowl. Cover and chill for at least one hour. Serve on bed of shredded lettuce.

Ensalada de Verduras
(Vegetable Salad)

Dressing: 1/2 cup OIL
1/4 cup LEMON JUICE
2 tsp. SUGAR
1 tsp. SALT
1/2 tsp. ground CUMIN
1 clove GARLIC

Blend together oil, lemon juice, sugar, salt and cumin. Spear garlic on toothpicks and let stand in mixture for at least 2 hours. Remove garlic.

Salad: 6 lg. TOMATOES
2 CUCUMBERS,
peeled and sliced
2/3 cup minced ONION
1 GREEN BELL PEPPER, diced
1 can (4 oz.) chopped OLIVES

An hour before serving, cut tomatoes in 3/4" chunks and mix with remaining salad ingredients. Add dressing and marinate for 1 hour.

Sopaipillas
(Puffy Fritters)

1 3/4 cups FLOUR
2 tsp. BAKING POWDER
1 tsp. SALT
2 Tbsp. SHORTENING
2/3 cup cold WATER

Sift flour, baking powder and salt into mixing bowl. Add shortening and cut in coarsely. Add water gradually. Mix just enough to hold together. Place on lightly floured board and knead until smooth. Cover and let rest about five minutes. Roll out to about 12" x 15" (dough should be about 1/8 inch thick). Cut into 3-inch squares or triangles. Drop a few at a time into very hot oil. Turn several times so that they will puff evenly and become golden brown. Serve with honey; your favorite fruit compote, or fill with beans and chiles.

Mexican Spoon Bread

1 can (15 oz.) CREAM-STYLE CORN
1 cup CORN MEAL
1/3 cup melted SHORTENING
2 EGGS, beaten
1 tsp. SALT
1/2 tsp. BAKING SODA
1 can (4 oz.) diced GREEN
    CHILES, drained
1 1/2 cups shredded LONGHORN CHEESE

    Combine first six ingredients; mix well. Pour half of the batter into a greased 9 x 9 x 2 pan. Sprinkle top with chiles and half of the cheese. Add remaining batter. Top with remaining cheese. Bake at 400° for 45 minutes. Cool 10 minutes before cutting into serving pieces. Serve with salsa on the side.

Pan de Frijoles
(Bean Bread)

2 tbsp. HONEY
1/4 cup HOT WATER
2 Tbsp. plus 3/4 tsp. ACTIVE
    DRY YEAST
10 to 12 cups WHOLE WHEAT FLOUR

2 cups cooked PINTO
    BEANS, puréed
1 1/2 cups cooked OATS
1 Tbsp. SALT
1/4 cup OIL

Stir honey into hot water. Let cool to lukewarm. Sprinkle in yeast and mix to dissolve. Stir in 1 tablespoon of flour, cover and set aside for 10 minutes. In a large bowl, combine beans, oats, salt and oil. Add yeast mixture. Stir in enough whole wheat flour to form a stiff dough. Place dough on a floured surface and knead until dough is smooth and elastic (about 15 minutes). Oil hands and rub over surface of dough. Cut into 4 equal pieces, cover with towels and allow to rise for 45 minutes to 1 hour. Lightly oil 4 bread pans and place loaf shaped dough in pans. Preheat oven to 375° and bake loaves about 45 minutes. Cool on wire racks.

Enchilada Casserole

1 lg. ONION, chopped
2 Tbsp. OIL
2 lbs. ground CHILI MEAT
1 can (16 oz.) TOMATOES
2 cans (8 oz. ea.) TOMATO
    SAUCE
1 tsp. SUGAR
2 tsp. ground CUMIN
2 tsp. PAPRIKA
2 lg. cloves GARLIC, crushed

1 can BEER
2 fresh JALAPEÑO PEPPERS,
    finely minced
5 Tbsp. CHILI POWDER
SALT and CAYENNE
    PEPPER to taste
2 cups grated LONGHORN
    CHEESE
1/2 cup chopped ONION
CORN TORTILLAS

Sauté onion in oil. Add chili meat and stir until gray. Add remaining ingredients and cook until thick (about 1 1/2 hours). Layer warm chili with grated cheese, onions and corn tortillas in a baking dish. Bake at 350° for 15-20 minutes.

Chile Verde con Carne
(Green Chile Stew with Meat)

1 sm. (2 1/2 - 3 lb.) POT ROAST
2 Tbsp. COOKING OIL
3/4 cup TOMATO JUICE
1 sm. ONION, finely chopped
1 clove GARLIC, chopped
1 tsp. OREGANO

1 tsp. SALT
1/4 tsp. PEPPER
1 Tbsp. FLOUR
1 can (14 oz.) TOMATOES
1 can (4 oz.) diced GREEN
CHILES

Brown roast in oil in a Dutch oven. Drain fat. Pour tomato juice over roast and bring to boiling; reduce heat. Cover and simmer for 1 hour. Shred meat and set aside. Add onion, garlic and spices to meat liquid and simmer for 10 minutes. Make a paste of flour and water and add to mixture. Add tomatoes, chiles and meat. Simmer for 10-15 minutes.

Chicken Enchiladas

Sauce:
- 2 cups TOMATO SAUCE
- 2 cups WATER
- 4 tsp. DRIED ONIONS
- 2 BOUILLON CUBES
- 1 tsp. GARLIC POWDER
- 1 tsp. OREGANO

Enchiladas:
- 12 CORN TORTILLAS
- 2 cups cooked CHICKEN
- 3 GREEN ONIONS, chopped
- shredded LETTUCE
- 1 pint SOUR CREAM
- 1/2 lb. grated MONTEREY JACK
- 2 Tbsp. chopped GREEN CHILES

Combine sauce ingredients and simmer for 5 minutes. Dip tortilla lightly in a small amount of hot oil. Drain. Dip tortilla in sauce, remove and fill with chicken, onions and lettuce. Roll up and place in casserole dish, seam down. Spoon balance of sauce over all; add dollops of sour cream, and sprinkle with cheese and chiles. Heat for 20 minutes in 350° oven.

Beef Tacos

1 lb. HAMBURGER
1 can (12 oz.) CORNED BEEF
1 ONION, diced
2 cups diced (small) POTATOES
1 can TOMATO SAUCE

CORN TORTILLAS
grated CHEESE
shredded LETTUCE
chopped TOMATOES

Fry hamburger and potatoes together and set aside. Sauté onion in hamburger drippings and drain. Add tomato sauce, hamburger and potatoes to onion mixture and combine. Place a portion of mixture in center of corn tortilla. Fold tortilla in half and secure top edges shut with a toothpick. Fry tortillas in hot oil on both sides until golden brown. Remove toothpick and fill with cheese, lettuce and tomatoes. Serve with taco sauce.

Tamales

- **24 CORN HUSKS** • **TAMALE DOUGH** • **TAMALE FILLING**

Cover cornhusks with warm water and soak until softened; drain. Spread center of corn leaves (lengthwise) with ***Tamale Dough*** and layer with a tablespoon of ***Tamale Filling.*** Roll, tucking in the tip end of the corn husk. Layer in steamer and steam until done (about 40 minutes).

Tamale Dough

1/2 cup LARD
2 lbs. MASA HARINA

2 tsp. SALT
3/4 cup WATER

Beat lard until light and fluffy. Mix with balance of ingredients. (A spoonful of dough should float to top of a cup of cold water. If it does not float, add water and continue beating.)

(Continued on next page)

*(**Tamales** continued from previous page)*

Tamale Filling

1/4 cup FLOUR
1 Tbsp. OIL
1/4 cup CHILI POWDER
1/2 cup TOMATO SAUCE
1 cup WATER
1 tsp. SALT
2 cups cooked, diced CHICKEN

Heat oil and add flour to brown. Add chili powder and mix; add tomato sauce. Add water slowly and stir. Add salt and simmer until sauce is thickened. Add chicken (or shredded beef). Cool thoroughly before spreading on tamale dough.

Salsa Fria and
Barbecued Rib Steaks

1 cup chopped TOMATOES
1/2 cup coarsely chopped ONIONS
1 can (4 oz.) diced GREEN CHILES
1 Tbsp. OLIVE OIL
1 Tbsp. VINEGAR
1 tsp. ground CORIANDER
1/4 tsp. SALT
1/4 tsp. PEPPER
4 boneless RIB STEAKS

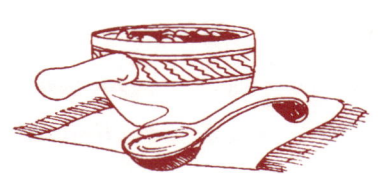

Combine all ingredients (except steaks), chill and serve very cold with hot barbecued steaks. Makes 2 cups *Salsa Fria.*

Frijoles de Ranchero

(Ranch Beans)

1 lb. dried PINTO BEANS
6 to 8 PORK CHOPS
1/4 lb. SALT PORK, diced
1 ONION, chopped

1 clove GARLIC, minced
1 Tbsp. CHILI POWDER
1 tsp. SALT
PEPPER to taste

Cover beans with water and soak overnight. Drain and rinse well. Place beans in a large saucepan, cover with water and bring to a boil. Reduce heat and simmer until beans are almost tender (about 2 hours). Brown pork chops in a skillet and set aside. Add salt pork to the skillet and fry until lightly browned. Add onion and garlic and sauté. Remove skillet from heat and stir in chili powder, salt and pepper. Add mixture to beans, stirring well. Arrange pork chops on top of beans, cover and simmer 45 minutes.

Chili Con Carne

2 lbs. GROUND BEEF or 1 lb. cubed ROUND STEAK
SALT and PEPPER
GARLIC SALT
1 cup chopped CELERY (with leaves)
3 cans (16 oz. ea.) TOMATOES
2 cans (6 oz. ea.) TOMATO PASTE
2 Tbsp. SUGAR
1 can (15 oz.) PINTO BEANS

1/2 cup PARSLEY
1 Tbsp. WORCESTERSHIRE
1 can BLACK OLIVES, pitted and quartered
1 BAY LEAF
1 GREEN BELL PEPPER, chopped
1/2 cup chopped ONION

Seasonings: CHILI POWDER, CAYENNE PEPPER, TABASCO® SAUCE, and OREGANO

Sprinkle beef with salt, pepper and garlic salt and sauté with celery in margarine. Cover and simmer 10 minutes, stirring occasionally. Add balance of ingredients (except seasonings) and simmer 5 to 10 minutes. Add seasonings to taste. Refrigerate overnight. Remove bay leaf before serving.

Chili Beef

1 can (19 oz.) RED CHILI SAUCE　　**2 lbs. lean boneless BEEF**
1 can (14.5 oz.) BEEF BROTH　　　　**cut into 1/2" pieces**

Combine chili sauce with bouillon and simmer beef in a covered saucepan for 45 - 60 minutes. Serve with beans or rice.

Chili Beef Tortilla Casserole

10-12 FLOUR TORTILLAS
1/2 cup grated CHEDDAR CHEESE
1/2 cup chopped GREEN ONIONS

Prepare *Chili Beef* recipe above. Place sauce in a shallow baking dish. Roll meat in flour tortillas and place seam side down in sauce. Sprinkle with cheese and onions and heat 10-15 minutes at 350°.

Mexican Cabbage Rolls

• 1 med. CABBAGE   • BEEF MIXTURE   • TOMATO SAUCE

Core cabbage. Place in a saucepan, cover with water and boil until outer leaves are limp and can be peeled off. Place about a tablespoon of ***Beef Mixture*** on each cabbage leaf. Roll and tuck in the ends. Place cabbage rolls in a shallow baking dish. Pour ***Tomato Sauce*** over all and cover and bake at 350° for 20 to 30 minutes.

Beef Mixture

2 lbs. GROUND BEEF
2 cups cooked RICE
2 tsp. SALT
1/2 tsp. PEPPER
1 can (4 oz.) diced GREEN CHILES

pinch SAVORY
pinch BASIL
pinch MARJORAM
1 Tbsp. CARAWAY SEED
1/2 tsp. grated LEMON PEEL

Combine all ingredients and set aside.

(Continued on next page)

*(**Cabbage Rolls** continued from previous page)*

Tomato Sauce

1 Tbsp. OIL
1 lg. ONION, chopped
6 lg. TOMATOES, diced
1 Tbsp. SUGAR
1 1/2 tsp. SALT

1/2 tsp. PEPPER
1/4 tsp. ROSEMARY
2 Tbsp. BROWN SUGAR
1/4 cup LEMON JUICE

Sauté onion in oil. Add balance of ingredients, cover and simmer until tomatoes are tender (about 20 minutes.)

Stuffed Bell Peppers

4 GREEN BELL PEPPERS
BEEF MIXTURE (see page 38)
TOMATO SAUCE (see page 39)
1/2 cup BREAD CRUMBS
1/2 cup grated LONGHORN CHEESE

Combine ingredients in *Beef Mixture* except for caraway seed and lemon peel. Combine ingredients in *Tomato Sauce* except for brown sugar and lemon juice. Wash bell peppers, slice in half lengthwise and remove seeds. Steam 10-15 minutes. Stuff with meat mixture and top with sauce. Sprinkle breadcrumbs and cheese over top and bake at 350° for 20 minutes.

Enchiladas Sabrosos

(Savory Enchiladas)

2 cans (10 3/4 oz. ea.) CREAM OF MUSHROOM SOUP
2 ctns. (16 oz. ea.) SOUR CREAM
1/3 cup MILK
24 CORN TORTILLAS
2 cans (7 oz. ea.) diced GREEN CHILES
2 bunches chopped GREEN ONIONS
2 cups shredded CHEDDAR CHEESE

Combine soup, sour cream and milk in a saucepan. Stir over medium heat until mixture boils then set aside. Soften tortillas by dipping into hot oil and drain on paper towels. Place 1/2 cup soup mixture in the bottom of a baking dish. Add a layer of tortillas on top, then layer the soup mixture, chiles, onions and cheese and continue layering. Top with a layer of the soup mixture and bake in a pre-heated 350° oven for 10 to 15 minutes. Serves 6 to 8.

Chalupa para Tostadas y Burros

(Pork Filling for Tostadas and Burros)

3 lbs. PORK ROAST
1 lb. PINTO BEANS, washed
2 cloves GARLIC, chopped
2 Tbsp. CHILI POWDER

1 Tbsp. ground CUMIN
1 Tbsp. OREGANO
1 can (4 oz.) diced GREEN CHILES
1 Tbsp. SALT

Place all ingredients in a large pot and cover with water. Simmer over low heat, adding water if needed, for 6 hours. Remove bones and shred meat. Continue cooking (no cover), until mixture is thick in texture. Serve on tostada shells with chopped lettuce, onion, tomatoes, avocado and cheese on the side. Or, roll mixture up in a warm flour tortilla like a burro. Chalupa freezes perfectly!

Burros de Chile Verde

2 lbs. ROUND STEAKS, diced
1 lg. ONION, diced
3 cloves GARLIC, diced
1 tsp. GARLIC POWDER
1 tsp. SALT
1 tsp. CUMIN
1/2 tsp. BLACK PEPPER
1 can (4 oz.) diced GREEN CHILES, drained
1 jar (16 oz.) GREEN CHILE SALSA
10 (10") FLOUR TORTILLAS

Place first seven ingredients in a crockpot. Cook on medium heat for 12 hours, or until meat is tender. Add chiles and salsa 30 minutes before serving. Add meat mixture to warmed tortillas. Fold tortillas burro style and serve with salsa on the side.

Fajitas de Pollo
(Chicken Fajitas)

1 lb. CHICKEN BREASTS, cut into strips

Marinade:

1 Tbsp. GARLIC SALT	1/4 cup LIME JUICE
1 tsp. fresh CILANTRO, chopped	1 Tbsp. WORCESTERSHIRE
2 tsp. BROWN SUGAR	SAUCE
1 Tbsp. VEGETABLE OIL	1/2 cup WATER
1/2 tsp. ground CUMIN	

Combine all ingredients in a large bowl, add chicken strips, cover and marinate for 2 hours in refrigerator.

Fajitas:

1 RED BELL PEPPER	1 lg. ONION
1 GREEN BELL PEPPER	12 (6") FLOUR TORTILLAS

Cut vegetables into strips and sauté in a large skillet. Add meat and cook, stirring constantly, until meat is done. Serve with tortillas, beans, grated cheese, sour cream, etc.

Arroz y Frijoles
(Rice and Beans)

6 slices BACON
1/2 cup chopped RED ONION
1/2 cup diced BELL PEPPER
1/2 cup sliced CELERY
1 cup uncooked RICE
1/2 tsp. OREGANO
1/2 tsp. SWEET BASIL
1 tsp. SALT

1/2 tsp. PEPPER
1 tsp. CHILI POWDER
1 cube BEEF BOUILLON
1 can (16 oz.) diced TOMATOES
2 tsp. SOY SAUCE
1 tsp. PARSLEY FLAKES
1 can (15 oz.) KIDNEY BEANS

Fry bacon until crisp; set aside. Sauté onion, pepper and celery in drippings. Add rice and spices and brown. Dissolve bouillon cube in tomato liquid, soy sauce and boiling water to measure 1 1/2 cups. Drain kidney beans and combine with all ingredients (except bacon). Place in an oven proof dish. Cover and bake 35 minutes at 350°. Fluff with fork and return to oven, uncovered, an additional 10 minutes. Stir in diced bacon.

Chiles Rellenos

2 cans (4 oz. ea.) whole GREEN CHILES or 8 fresh GREEN CHILES*
1 lb. MONTEREY JACK CHEESE, sliced
4 EGGS, separated

4 Tbsp. BUTTER
FLOUR
1 cup grated MONTEREY JACK CHEESE

Slit chiles lengthwise and fill centers with slices of cheese. Beat together; one egg yolk for every two chiles; one tablespoon of hot water and 1 tablespoon of flour for each egg. Beat egg whites until they form soft peaks. Fold into egg yolk mixture.

Roll chiles in flour and then dip into egg mixture. Heat butter in a skillet and brown chiles on all sides. Drain on paper towels and place in a shallow baking dish. Cover with *Chiles Rellenos Sauce* and top with grated cheese. Heat in 325° oven for 15 minutes.

(Continued on next page)

(Chiles Rellenos continued from previous page)

Chiles Rellenos Sauce

2 Tbsp. OIL
2 ONIONS, chopped
3 cloves GARLIC
2 Tbsp. FLOUR

1 can (6 oz.) TOMATO PASTE
1/2 tsp. OREGANO
1/2 cup WATER
1/2 tsp. SALT

Sauté onions and garlic until golden brown. Stir in balance of ingredients. Cook until mixture thickens to gravy-like consistency.

Hint: Prepare rellenos and sauce in advance and store in refrigerator. When ready to use, add grated cheese and heat in 325° oven for 30 minutes.

*Place fresh peppers over open flame until brown. Wrap in damp cloth to steam for five minutes. Remove peel, seeds and veins.

Eggplant de Mexico

1 lb. EGGPLANT
1 sm. ONION, chopped
1/2 tsp. SALT
2 cups chopped fresh TOMATOES
1/2 cup finely chopped ONION
1 clove GARLIC, minced
1/2 tsp. SALT

1 can (4 oz.) diced GREEN
   CHILES
1/4 tsp. SWEET BASIL
2 EGGS, beaten
1 cup grated MONTEREY
   JACK CHEESE

Peel and cut eggplant into 1" cubes. Cook with onion in boiling salted water for 10 minutes. Drain. Combine the rest of ingredients (except cheese). Place all ingredients into an oiled 1 1/2 qt. casserole. Cover and bake in 375° oven for 1/2 hour. Remove cover and reduce heat to 350°. Sprinkle cheese on top and continue to bake until cheese is bubbly. Serves 4.

Fried Eggplant

Pare **EGGPLANT** and cut into 1/4" slices crosswise. Sprinkle with **SALT**, **GARLIC SALT** and **PEPPER**. Beat **ONE EGG** with **2 Tbsp. MILK**. Coat slices with **FLOUR** and dip them in the egg mixture. Roll in fine, dry **BREAD CRUMBS** and fry in hot **OLIVE OIL** until golden. Drain and serve.

Frijoles Refritos con Queso

1 Tbsp. **LARD**
2 cups cooked, mashed **BEANS**

1 Tbsp. **FLOUR**
grated **CHEESE**

Heat lard. Add 1 tablespoon flour and brown. Add beans, stir and bring to simmer. Place in casserole dish, sprinkle with cheese and heat until cheese bubbles. Serve with tortilla chips and salsa.

Calabacitas con Puerco

(Squash with Pork)

2 lbs. fresh ZUCCHINI or SUMMER SQUASH
1 can (4 oz.) diced GREEN CHILES
1 sm. cooked PORK ROAST, shredded
1 can (15 1/4 oz.) WHOLE KERNEL CORN
1/2 lb. grated LONGHORN CHEESE

Cut squash into small pieces. Boil until tender (about 15 minutes) in salted water. Combine with chiles, pork and corn in a greased casserole dish. Sprinkle cheese over top and place in preheated oven at 400° until cheese melts.

Mexicali Garbanzos

2 cans (16 oz. ea.) GARBANZO BEANS, drained
1 RED ONION, thinly sliced
1 GREEN BELL PEPPER, diced

1 RED BELL PEPPER, diced
1/4 cup sliced BLACK OLIVES
1 can (4 oz.) diced GREEN CHILES

Toss all ingredients together in a large bowl. Add *Mexicali Dressing* and toss well again.

Mexicali Dressing

1 clove GARLIC, minced
3 Tbsp. OLIVE OIL
4 Tbsp. VINEGAR

1/2 tsp. SALT
1/4 tsp. BLACK PEPPER
1/2 tsp. crushed OREGANO

Combine all ingredients in a jar. Cover and shake vigorously until thoroughly mixed.

Fruit Empanadas

3 cups FLOUR
2 tsp. BAKING POWDER
1/2 tsp. SALT
3 Tbsp. SUGAR
1/2 cup SHORTENING
1/2 cup MILK

Sift and mix dry ingredients. Cut in shortening. Knead with hands, adding enough milk to hold dough together. Roll dough out to 1/8-inch thickness. Cut into circles (about a dozen). Place two tablespoons of fruit mixture (apple, pumpkin etc.) on one half. Moisten edges of dough with cold water and fold empanada in half. Seal edges together with tines of a fork. Bake at 350° about 25 minutes. Sprinkle with confectioners sugar.

Flan

1 3/4 cups SUGAR
3 EGG WHITES
8 EGG YOLKS
2 cans EVAPORATED MILK
2 tsp. VANILLA

Melt one cup of the sugar over very low heat. Pour into a mold, tilting to make sure that melted sugar covers bottom and sides of pan completely. Allow to cool.

In a bowl, beat eggs and add milk, the remaining sugar and vanilla. Pour into the sugar-lined mold. Place mold in a pan of water in 350° oven for about 1 1/4 hours, or until knife inserted in the center comes out clean. Cool a few minutes, then turn onto a plate. Refrigerate for several hours before serving.

Dulce Mexicano
(Mexican Candy)

2 cups SUGAR
1/4 cup WATER
1 cup EVAPORATED MILK

pinch of SALT
2 tsp. grated ORANGE PEEL

Add sugar to skillet over medium heat and stir with wooden spoon until caramelized. Add water. Stir until sugar dissolves. Add remaining sugar, milk, and salt. Place over low heat and stir until mixture boils. Cook, stirring constantly, until mixture reaches soft ball stage. Remove from heat and cool to lukewarm (do not stir). Add orange peel. Beat until candy loses gloss and holds its shape when dropped from a spoon. Pour into lightly buttered 8-inch square pan. Cut when cool.

Mexican Wedding Cakes

1 cup softened BUTTER
1/2 cup POWDERED SUGAR
1 tsp. VANILLA
2 1/4 cups all-purpose FLOUR
1/4 tsp. SALT
1 cup finely chopped NUTS

Cream butter until light and fluffy. Add sugar and vanilla and mix thoroughly. Add flour, salt and nuts and mix well. Shape into walnut-sized balls. Place balls on ungreased baking sheet in 325° oven for 20 to 30 minutes (do not allow to become brown). Roll cakes in powdered sugar; cool, roll again in powdered sugar.

Almendrado
(Almond Pudding)

1 1/2 env. unflavored GELATIN
1/2 cup cold WATER
1/4 cup boiling WATER
6 EGG WHITES
1/2 cup SUGAR

1/2 tsp. VANILLA
1/2 tsp. ALMOND EXTRACT
pinch SALT
RED and GREEN FOOD
    COLORING

Soak gelatin in cold water. Add boiling water to dissolve. Cool. Beat egg whites until stiff. Using an electric mixer on high speed, gradually add sugar and gelatin liquid. Add vanilla, almond flavoring and salt and combine thoroughly. Divide mixture into three parts. Leave one part white, tint the other parts red and green. Pour the green colored mixture into a loaf pan lined with waxed paper. Add the white and then the red layers. Chill at least 4 hours and serve with *Almendrado Custard Sauce.*

(Continued on next page)

(**Almendrado** continued from previous page)

Almendrado Custard Sauce

2 Tbsp. CORNSTARCH
1 Tbsp. cold MILK
3 cups scalded MILK
1/2 cup SUGAR
pinch of SALT

6 EGG YOLKS
1/2 tsp. VANILLA
1/2 tsp. ALMOND EXTRACT
1/2 cup sliced, toasted ALMONDS

Dissolve cornstarch in cold milk. In a saucepan, combine scalded milk, sugar and salt. Add cornstarch mixture. Boil until slightly thickened, stirring constantly. Beat egg yolks, vanilla and almond extract together. Add to hot mixture slowly, stirring constantly until mixture is slightly thickened (about one minute). Chill. Serve slices of **Almendrado** topped with custard sauce and a sprinkle of almonds.

Capirotada
(Bread Pudding)

3 EGGS, beaten
2 1/2 oz. MILK
3 Tbsp. BROWN SUGAR
2 tsp. CINNAMON
8 slices toasted BREAD
1/2 cup toasted, chopped ALMONDS

1/2 cup chopped PECANS
1/2 cup chopped WALNUTS
1/2 cup RAISINS
1 APPLE, sliced thin
1 cup JACK CHEESE, cubed

Combine eggs, milk, sugar and cinnamon in a bowl. Combine balance of ingredients in another bowl. Place 4 of the bread slices in a buttered baking dish. Pour half of the milk mixture over bread and add a layer of half of the nut mixture. Add another layer of bread and the balance of the nut mixture. Top with *Capirotada Syrup* and bake for 25 minutes in a preheated 350° oven.

(Continued on next page)

*(**Capirotada** continued from previous page)*

Capirotada Syrup

2 cups BROWN SUGAR
2 cups WATER

1 tsp. VANILLA

Combine sugar, water and vanilla in a saucepan and bring to a boil. Lower heat and simmer 15 minutes or until slightly thickened.

Dulcitas

12 CORN TORTILLAS
1/2 cup POWDERED SUGAR
 (or 1/3 cup granulated)

2 tsp. CINNAMON
1/2 tsp. COCOA

Soften corn tortillas in heated oil. Stack and cut into eight pie-shaped pieces. Cook tortilla pieces in heated oil until crisp but not brown. Drain. Mix sugar, cinnamon and cocoa in a paper sack or plastic bag. Add tortilla pieces and shake to coat evenly.

Polvarones de Lemón

(Lemon Sugar Cookies)

2 cups FLOUR
1 tsp. BAKING POWDER
1/2 tsp. SALT
1/2 cup BUTTER

1 cup SUGAR
1 EGG
1 Tbsp. grated LEMON RIND
1 Tbsp. LEMON JUICE

Sift together flour, baking powder and salt. Cream butter and add sugar, egg, lemon rind and juice. Beat until light and fluffy. Add dry ingredients and stir until completely mixed. Wrap dough in plastic and chill in refrigerator for at least an hour. Roll dough out to 1/8" thickness and cut cookies with cooky cutter. Place on an ungreased baking sheet, sprinkle with sugar and bake in 375° oven until edges are lightly browned (about 8 minutes). Cool on wire rack. Makes 36 cookies.

Horchata de Melón

(Melon Drink)

2 cups washed and dried MELON SEEDS
2 qts. WATER
2 cups SUGAR
grated rind of 1 LEMON
1 CINNAMON STICK

Grind melon seeds. Combine with balance of ingredients and refrigerate overnight. Strain and stir thoroughly. Serve in tall chilled glasses over crushed ice.

Chocolate de Mexico

1 STICK CINNAMON STICK
6 cups MILK
1 tsp. VANILLA
6 squares unsweetened, grated CHOCOLATE
1 EGG, separated

Place cinnamon stick, milk and vanilla in a saucepan. Bring to a simmer and add chocolate. Add egg yolk and stir rapidly. Beat egg white until stiff and fold into mixture. Sweeten to taste.

Simply Sensational™
Cook Books

"Mini-sized" cookbooks packed with savory recipes! Give your tastebuds a treat with authentic recipes that are both flavorful and easy to make. These books are great for personal use and make wonderful gifts!

Each attractive 5 1/2" x 4" book has 64 pages and is comb bound for lay flat use. All books only $4.95 each!

For a free catalog of Golden West cookbooks call 1-800-658-5830

chili institute.com